Juicing Guide

Top Juicing Recipes that Make Juicing for Weight Loss Easy

Martina Richardson

Table of Contents

CHAPTER 5: YOUR 7 DAY JUICING DIET MEAL PLAN.85

Introduction

More than likely, you have heard all about juicing and juicing diets. However, you may not be familiar with the truth about juicing, especially when it comes to juicing and weight loss. Many people try to start a juicing diet without actually learning what juicing is all about, how long they should being on a juice-only diet and the benefits that juicing has to offer.

If you have considered juicing for weight loss, this guide is for you. This juicing guide offers helpful information on juice, the benefits of juicing and so much more. You will even find some great tips that will make your juice diet even more successful. The best part about this juicing guide is that it is packed with the tastiest, healthiest juicing recipes out there. Whether you enjoy vegetable flavored juices or you like the sweeter juices, you are sure to find great recipes that will fit with your tastes and your lifestyle. Many of the recipes included are very easy to make, especially with the help of a quality juicer.

Do not start your juicing diet until you read this guide. With this guide by your side, you can begin juicing for weight loss, armed with important information and great recipes. Even when you stop juicing for every meal, you can go back to this guide for great juicing recipes that can be used anytime for a great dose of vitamins and minerals.

Chapter 1: What is the Juicing?

Before you begin juicing for weight loss, it is important to know more about juicing and how it works. What is juicing? Juicing is simply defined as the process of extracting juices from vegetable of fruit plant tissues. Juicing can be done in several different ways. Some fruits can be juiced by hand, but to get the most juice from most fruits and vegetables, a good juicer is needed.

Many people choose to juice fruits and vegetables because it offers the body many important nutrients in a way that can easily be assimilated by the body. When juicing fruits and veggies at home with a domestic juicer, the produce is prepared and then pushed through the feeding chamber of the juicer. Then the machine uses either a separation or pureeing process to juice the produce.

In most cases, you do not need to peel produce before putting it through the juicer. However, some fruits and vegetables may be exceptions. For example, oranges and other citrus fruits happen to have bitter oils in their peels, which is why it is best to peel them before they are juiced. Fruits and vegetables with a very hard rind, such as squash, pumpkins, watermelon and other similar items of produce will need to have the peel or rind removed to avoid damaging the juicer.

One of the main reasons that juicing has become so popular is because taking in fresh, raw produce is actually much better than taking in vegetables that have been cooked. The juices help to remove toxins and waste from the body, also working to regenerate and repair body tissues. Fresh juices also provide plenty of important enzymes and antioxidants to the body, which can help to improve metabolism, help along metabolic processes and eliminate free radicals within the body.

Juicing not only helps to preserve the important nutrients found in veggies and fruits, but it also allows individuals to take in more produce at one time than they could if they were eating it. A large glass of fruit or vegetable juice includes the juice of more fruits and veggies than you could ever eat at one time.

Of course, while many people can definitely benefit from a juicing diet, it is always a good idea to talk to your doctor before starting any new diet. People who may be taking prescription medications or dealing with an illness need to talk to their doctor before drinking a large quantity of juice, since juices may change the way their body metabolizes the medications they are taking.

For most healthy individuals, juicing provides a healthy, safe way to begin increasing the intake of important nutrients. Even juicing for one meal a day can provide great results.

While some people choose to only juice for one meal each day, others decide to go on a juice diet for a few days where they only take in juices. This may be okay for a few days, but a diet of only juices is usually not a good idea for more than a few days at a time. For the best results, you can drink only juices for a few days and then you can go back to eating a regular healthy diet while drinking a glass of juice for one of your meals each day.

Chapter 2: Benefits of Juicing

Before you decide to start juicing for weight loss, you may want to take a closer look at the benefits juicing can offer you. Juicing has become quite popular because of the many benefits to it. Maybe you have heard other people talk about how great juicing is but wondered if it really can help you. Here is a look at some of the top benefits you can enjoy when you try the juicing diet yourself.

Benefit #1 – Efficiently Consume Large Amounts of Fruits and Veggies

One of the main benefits of juicing is that it allows you to efficiently consume large amounts of fruits and veggies. You should be getting more than five servings of fruits and vegetables each day. The problem is that most people never get that many servings of fruits and veggies. It can be difficult to fit all those fruits and veggies into your meals each day. However, juicing makes it a lot easier for you to get all the fruits and vegetables that your body really needs. In fact, you could actually get all the recommended servings of fruits and veggies in a single glass of juice. This makes it fast and convenient to begin adding more healthy produce to your life on a regular basis.

Benefit #2 – Include a Wide Variety of Fruits and Veggies in Your Diet

Another great benefit of juicing for weight loss is the ability to include a wide variety of fruits and veggies in your diet. If you are eating vegetables and fruits regularly, it is easy to get into a rut. Soon you may find that you are eating the same fruits and veggies on a regular basis. This means that you may not be getting the wide variety of vitamins and minerals that are needed by your body. When you begin juicing, you can include a wider variety of great fruits and veggies in your juices, making sure that you get a wide variety of different nutrients that your body needs.

Some people find that they do not particularly like the flavor of certain fruits and vegetables. When you begin juicing, you can enjoy the benefits of fruits or veggies you do not like as much without having to taste them. Many times you can add certain veggies or fruits to a juice with another fruit or vegetable that has a predominant flavor, overpowering the flavor of the item you do not like. You do not have to avoid certain veggies and fruits just because you do not like their flavor. You can easily add them to juices and get all their benefits without tasting them specifically.

Benefit #3 – Enjoy More Energy

One of the greatest benefits that people often notice after they begin juicing is that they enjoy more energy. One reason that you may experience more energy when juicing is because your body does not have to use very much energy to digest the veggie and fruit juices. The juicers are almost totally digested. You simply drink the juice and your body will not need to use much energy on digestion. Since you are saving all that energy, you will probably notice that your energy levels begin to increase.

Many people that do not get enough fruits and vegetables notice that they feel fatigued on a regular basis. If you are dealing with fatigue and the need to sleep more than usual, juicing may be able to help. After you begin juicing for a few days, you will quickly find that your energy levels begin to skyrocket, which can help improve your life in many different ways.

Benefit #4 – Get Plenty of Chlorophyll From Green Juices

Many of the juicing recipes that you will find in this juicing guide and in other places include produce that contains a lot of chlorophyll. You will especially find a large amount of chlorophyll in the greener juices that include a large amount of greens, such as spinach. Chlorophyll is a great detoxifier and is found naturally in plants. When you begin getting more chlorophyll in your diet, you will find that it helps to eliminate parasites from the body. It also strengthens your body, helps to rebuild your blood cells and helps purify and detoxify your body as well.

Benefit #5 – Detoxify Your Liver for Better Health

You will also find that juicing for weight loss can offer the benefit of detoxifying your liver for better health. Your liver has so many functions that it has to undertake on a regular basis and these functions are very important to the way your body works. One of the most important functions of your liver is to clean out the blood, removing metabolic waste and toxins from the blood. Since most people end up being exposed to many toxins on a regular basis, the liver needs to be in great shape so it can keep your blood as clean as possible.

Some of the best antioxidants that help to cleanse out your liver include vitamin C, beta carotene and vitamin E. Niacin and various B vitamins also help to cleanse the liver as well. Some great veggies that are known to be good for detoxifying the liver include cauliflower, Brussels sprouts and cabbage. Adding some of these veggies to your juices from time to time can help ensure you enjoy this benefit from your juicing.

Benefit #7 – Enjoy Healthier, More Beautiful Skin and Hair

When you begin juicing on a regular basis, you can also enjoy healthier, more beautiful skin and hair. For many people, this benefit is unexpected. When you begin juicing, you will be able to increase your intake of veggies and fruits that contain vitamin E and vitamin C. Both of these vitamins work to help protect your skin from damage when it is exposed to the sun. Some of the best fruits to use to get these vitamins include blueberries and blackberries. In fact, you'll find some recipes in this juicing guide that combine blueberries and blackberries, which can help you get the vitamins you need for healthier skin.

If you are not getting enough riboflavin in your diet, you can experience hair loss, cracked lips and a variety of different skin problems. Some of the veggies that have a lot of riboflavin in them include spinach and kale, which are found in many of the juicing recipes included. As you begin getting more of this important vitamin, you will notice that your skin begins to get healthier and the hair loss problem may begin to abate as well. Many other vitamins and minerals that you will get while juicing will help improve the health and appearance of your skin and hair as well.

Benefit #8 – Give Your Immune System a Boost

Since so many people today do not get the fruits and vegetables that their body needs, it is no wonder that so many people have weakened immune systems. When you begin juicing on a regular basis, you will enjoy the benefit of giving your immune system a great boost. If you get colds or other illnesses on a regular basis, juicing may be just the thing to help you feel a lot better.

When you begin juicing regularly, you will start getting a wide variety of different antioxidants, which are needed to keep your immune system functioning the way it should. Some of the important antioxidants you will get from veggies and fruits include vitamin E, vitamin A and vitamin C. Phytochemicals are also found in many fruits and vegetables and they come with a variety of great health benefits, giving your immune system and your overall health a good boost.

Benefit #9 – Prevent Cancer

One of the more famous benefits of juicing is the benefit of cancer prevention. Since juicing gives you a wide variety of vitamins, minerals and antioxidants that your body needs, it arms your body to fight off cancer cells. When you juice on a regular basis and ensure you are getting all those important nutrients, you will be going a long way towards reducing your risk of getting cancer in the future.

Interestingly enough, juicing is often recommended to individuals who already have cancer. While it does not miraculously cure cancer right away, the antioxidants help to fight off cancer cells and give the immune system a boost so the body can work to fight off cancer on its own. When used along with other treatments, it can be an excellent method of beating cancer. Of course, if you are being treated for cancer, it is always important to follow the advice of your doctors and make sure you talk to them about juicing to ensure you avoid doing anything that may interfere with other treatments you may be given for cancer.

Benefit #10 – Slow the Aging Process

Last, juicing for weight loss can actually have the benefit of slowing down the aging process. Instead of wasting your money on all those expensive anti-aging creams and lotions, nature can offer you a great anti-aging treatment – fruits and veggies. Drinking fresh juices on a regular basis can provide your body with the nutrients it needs to stay young. Since free radicals are known to cause aging, getting plenty of antioxidants from the juice you drink will help to fight off free radicals, slowing down the aging process. People that get plenty of fruits and vegetables on a regular basis are often able to look younger and they are less likely to deal with health problems that come with aging as well.

Of course, these are only a few of the great benefits you can enjoy when you begin juicing. Juicing may also help to improve heart health, since you are less likely to eat foods that may lead to high blood pressure, high cholesterol and heart disease in the future. Juicing can also help you to lose weight, which is one of the more popular benefits individuals want to experience when they go on a juicing diet. As you begin juicing, you will fill up on low calorie fruits and vegetables in juice form, which will keep you from indulging in other unhealthy foods. Juicing also helps to cleanse out your body, eliminating toxins and waste, which can help you to lose weight as well. Just a few of the other benefits of juicing may include reducing problems with depression, strengthening your bones, improving eye health, rebuilding blood cells, keeping your body pH less acidic and reducing your risk of many different diseases.

Chapter 3: Helpful Tips to Simplify Juicing for Weight Loss

When you begin juicing for weight loss, you want to make sure that you get the best results from your juicing diet. The good news is that there are some great tips out there that can make juicing simpler and tips that can help you ensure you get the best nutrition when you make and drink these juices. To get the tastiest juices and the most benefits from juicing, the following are some top tips to keep in mind as you begin juicing and using the recipes you will find in this book.

Tip #1 – Choose Organic Fruits and Veggies if Possible

One of the best tips to remember when you begin juicing is to choose organic fruits and veggies if possible. Going with organic fruits and veggies helps you avoid pesticides, which you do not want to take in when trying to get all the goodness you can from juicing. Of course, certain fruits and veggies are worse than others when it comes to pesticides. The following fruits and veggies may have thinner skins, which make them more vulnerable to pesticides, so it is better to choose organically grown versions of these items:

- Kale
- Carrots
- Blueberries
- Spinach
- Lettuces
- Cucumbers
- Blueberries
- Strawberries
- Celery
- Collard Greens

If the fruit or vegetable has a thin skin, it is a good idea to choose the organic version of the fruit or veggie when you plan to use them for juicing.

Tip #2 – Learn About Great Additions that Make Juices Taste Better

When you first start juicing, you may find that some of the juices do not taste very good to you, especially those that only have vegetables in them. While you will get used to the taste over time, you can add some simple additions to juices to make them taste better to you. Here are a few of the best additions to add to juices when you need something to make them more palatable for you.

- **Cranberries** – If you like the flavor of cranberries, they can be added to juices to make them taste a bit better. They work well in green juices, since the cranberry flavor usually overpowers the greens. Not only will the cranberries add great flavor, but they offer a huge amount of antioxidants and phytonutrients as well.

- **Coconut** – Unsweetened shredded coconut or fresh coconut can be used to offer some flavor to juices as well. Coconut water can also be added to juices to add flavor and dilute them just a bit. Coconut has healthy fats in it, so it tastes good and offers great health benefits too.

- **Fresh Ginger** – You may notice that many of the juice recipes included in this juicing guide include fresh ginger. This is because ginger adds some great flavor, especially to vegetable juices that may not taste as good. Ginger also works to reduce bad cholesterol levels and offers great cardiovascular health benefits as well.

- **Limes and Lemons** – Limes and lemons have powerful flavors, which makes them the perfect addition to juices when you want to make them taste a little more palatable. Simple add in half of a lime or a lemon to any juice to improve the flavor. Just make sure you peel the lime or lemon and remove the seeds.

Tip #3 – Always Drink Juices as Soon as You Can Once You Juice Fruits and Veggies

One of the most important tips you can follow as you start juicing is to always drink juices as soon as you can one you have juiced the fruits and veggies. As time goes by, the juice will begin to lose some of its nutritional value. Sometimes the juice will turn a strange color as it begins to oxidize as well, although this does not mean that the juice has gone bad. It is best to drink the juice immediately. If you cannot drink the juice immediately, work to make sure you drink the juice within 24 hours for the best nutrition and taste. Fresh juices do not have any preservatives in them, so they can quickly go bad.

Tip #4 – Try Prepping Produce in Advance for Faster Juicing

Many people avoid juicing because they think that juicing will require a lot of work and time. Juicing actually can take quite a bit of your time, since you have to wash and cut up veggies and fruits before you can juice many of them. Since it can be easy to go off your juicing diet because it all feels like too much work, you may want to try prepping your produce in advance for faster juicing. Try preparing produce by washing it and cutting it up. You can do this a couple times a week so ingredients for juices are readily available. Simple place prepared produce in storage containers or plastic bags, then put them in the refrigerator. Then you can quickly get the ingredients out of the refrigerator and use them when needed. Of course, remember that veggies and fruits can start losing nutrients after you cut them, so if you prep ahead of time, avoid prepping veggies and fruits too far in advance so you avoid losing those important nutrients that your body needs.

Tip #5 – Clean Your Juicer Right Away and Clean Thoroughly

It is important that you clean your juicer right away, making sure that you clean it thoroughly. It is easy to put off cleaning the juicer because you are in a hurry, but this can quickly lead to big problems. If you do not quickly clean out the juice and pulp, it will begin to get sticky. This will make it even more difficult for you to get your juicer clean. If you have a high quality juicer, it should only take a few minutes to clean it when you are done juicing, which will save you a lot of time later on. If your juicer has a metal grater, one of the best tips for cleaning it is to keep a toothbrush around to get it clean.

Tip #6 – If You Do Store Juice, Store Carefully

While it is best to drink your juices quickly, you can store them. However, if you are going to store juices, make sure you store them carefully. Juices are best right away, but you can keep them stored for about 24 hours without too much of a problem. For the best results, make sure you place juice in a glass jar – avoid putting juice in a plastic container. Make sure that the jar has a lid that is airtight and fill the jar with juice right up to the top so you avoid having too much oxygen in the jar, which can damage your juice. Once you have the juice in the jar, make sure it is put in your refrigerator and keep it there until you are ready to drink the juice.

Tip #7 – Always Take the Time to Wash Produce

Always make sure you take the time to wash your produce thoroughly before you juice it. Fruit and vegetables may have contaminants on the outside, which you need to wash away to avoid contaminating your fruit. Even if you are going to remove the peeling or the rind, you still need to wash the produce well. Contamination can still occur if the skin or rind is removed.

Tip #8 – Avoid Peeling Fruits and Veggies that Can Be Eaten with the Skin

If you can eat the fruit or vegetable with the skin on, leave the skin on when you juice them. Many fruits and vegetables contain a large amount of nutrients within their skins, so removing the skins means that you are losing out on some great nutrition. For example, you can leave the skin on cucumbers, apples and even carrots when you are ready to juice them. Just make sure you wash them very well before juicing. Pay attention to the recipes within this juicing guide, since they will tell you when it is okay to leave the skin on the fruits or vegetables that go in the juice.

Tip #9 – Do Not Ruin Your Juice by Adding Sugar – There are Better Ways to Sweeten Juices

When you go on a juicing diet to lose weight, you are working to get away from sugar and processed foods. Do not ruin your juice by adding sugar to the juice if you think it needs a little sweetness. The great news is that there are many better ways that you can sweeten the juices a bit if you think they need it. For example, instead of sugar, a sugar alternative like Stevia, which happens to be all natural, can add some sweetness to the juice. A touch of honey can add some sweetness in a natural way as well. In many cases, just adding a sweet fruit to the juice can help you ensure that you get plenty of sweet flavor in the juice. There is never a need to add any sugar to these juice recipes.

Chapter 4: Delicious Juicing Recipes for Any Meal

If you're following the a juicing diet, you'll find that you can use juicing recipes for any meal or snack during the day. Juicing for weight loss can be extremely effective, but you want to ensure you have a wide variety of juices to enjoy so you don't get bored. The following are some wonderful recipes. Some include fruits, others are primarily made up of veggies and some even include both fruits and vegetables. You're sure to find some great juicing recipes that will tempt your taste buds while helping you lose some weight.

Orange Mango Juice Recipe

This juice combines together the delicious flavors of oranges and mangos. The addition of some kale leaves provides an extra nutritional punch when you consume this juice. You'll be able to make this juice very quickly and it's an especially tasty treat when you first get up in the morning. Add a little ice to make it extra cold and refreshing.

What You'll Need:

1 large mango
4 medium oranges
3-4 leaves of kale

How to Make It:

Wash the mango before using. Remove the skin from the mango, since some individuals may have a bad reaction to some of the chemicals naturally found in the mango's skin. Cut the pit of the mango out, then cut the mango into medium sized chunks.

Peel all four oranges. Break the oranges into 4-5 big sections that can easily be fed into the juice.

Was the kale leaves and shake them dry or dry with a
paper towel.

Place mango chunks, orange sections and kale leave in a
juice. Juice ingredients. Makes 1-2 servings. Drink
immediately for the best taste.

Refreshing Red Pepper and Basil Juice Recipe

Along with refreshing, tasty red bell pepper, this juice is packed with great veggies. It includes cucumbers, broccoli, carrot, celery and chia seeds, which pack in plenty of great nutrients. The basil really gives the flavor a boost, as does the lime. The tabasco adds a kick, but you can eliminate the tabasco if you don't like it.

What You'll Need:

1 large bunch of broccoli
1 handful of fresh basil leaves
1 carrot, small
1 small cucumber
1 red bell pepper, large
½ lime, with the rind
2 teaspoons of chia seeds
2 celery stalks
½ cup of Jicama with the skin
Tabasco sauce to taste (optional)

How to Make It:

Wash broccoli, basil leaves, carrot, cucumber, red bell pepper, celery and Jicama.

Remove pepper top, seeds and innards from the red bell pepper. Cut broccoli into chunks. Peel carrot and cut carrot into chunks. Leave peeling on cucumber but cut cucumber into chunks that will fit into your juicer. Chop celery into chunks as well.

Place broccoli, basil leaves, carrot, cucumber, bell pepper, lime, celery stalks and Jicama into the juicer. Juice until finished. Place juice in a bottle or pitcher. Add tabasco if desired and chia seeds. Mix well. Serve immediately.

Lime Spinach Juice Recipe

All the spinach in this juice offers many great nutrients your body needs, such as potassium and iron. The baby carrots add even more vitamins and minerals that are important. The lime and green apple added to the juice provide a delicious flavor that will make you wish you doubled this recipe.

What You'll Need:

1 medium green apple
1 large cucumber
5-6 baby carrots
2 large handfuls of spinach
1 lime

How to Make It:

Wash the green apple, cutting it into chunks, leaving skin on the apple. Wash cucumber and leave it's skin on too, cutting into chunks. Wash spinach carefully, allowing to drain in a colander. Wash lime, remove the skin and then cut up the lime into chunks.

Add apple chunks, cucumber chunks, carrots, spinach and lime chunks into the juicer. Juice the ingredients.

Serve juice right away.

NOTE: If you like your juice a bit sweeter, simply add another apple to the juice for some extra sweetness.

Wild Edible Greens Juice Recipe

If you have a lot of wild, edible greens around your home, these fresh greens can be added to your juice for a healthy, delicious juice. Just make sure you know which greens are edible, since you want to avoid eating anything that could be dangerous. Have fun finding out about fresh wild greens. You can look online or even buy a book that will help you to identify greens that you can eat.

What You'll Need:

½ cucumber
1 large lemon
1 ½ pounds of fresh wild greens (such as sow thistle, chick weed, yellow dock, dandelion or miner's lettuce)
1 inch piece of fresh ginger root
3-4 bok choy stalks
6 celery tops

How to Make It:

Start by washing all the fresh wile greens you have collected, allowing them to drain in a colander before using them in the juice. Wash cucumber, lemon, bok choy and celery tops as well. Leave the skin on the cucumber, cutting it up into pieces that will easily fit in your juicer. Chop bok choy stalks into smaller pieces and cut up celery tops if needed.

Add all ingredients to the juicer, juicing until complete. Makes about 24 ounces of wild edible greens juice, which is about two servings. Drink the juice immediately.

Tasty Morning Apple and Carrot Juice Recipe

This delicious juice is a wonderful juice to make in the morning for a great pick me up. It's tasty and packed with great nutrients to help fuel you through the day. The beet adds some great vitamins and minerals, but you won't taste it with the green apples in the juice, offering a nice sweet and tart flavor.

What You'll Need:

1/2 beet
2 medium green apples
1 stalk of celery with leaves
2 medium sized carrots

How to Make It:

Wash the apples, celery and carrots. Cut a beet in half, peeling carefully and cutting into chunks. Leave the peeling on the apples, but core the apple and then cut it into pieces. The celery should be cut up as well. Peel carrots, cutting into large pieces.

Place the beet, apples, celery and carrots into a juicer and then process. Serve the juice up right away for a great way to start the morning.

Carrot Citrus Twist Juice Recipe

The carrots in this delicious juice recipe pack great nutrients, offering one of the best ways to get vitamin A. Some of the other important minerals carrots provide include copper, potassium, calcium and iron. While carrot juice tastes great by itself, adding the citrus to the recipe really gives it a tangy, sweet twist. Not only do the oranges add great flavor, but they add a huge amount of vitamin C to your juice as well. Try this delicious juice recipe over ice. It makes a great juice to drink for breakfast.

What You'll Need:

2 large oranges, peeled and seeded
8 large carrots, unpeeled

How to Make It:

Start by peeling the oranges, making sure you remove any seeds. Break up the oranges into large sections so they will fit into your juicer.

Wash the carrots well, removing any dirt. However, leave the skin on the carrots, since the skin is packed with great nutrients. Cut the tops off the carrots. Cut carrots into chunks.

Place oranges and carrots into the juicer, juicing. Makes 2 glasses of juice.

Tangy Grapefruit Carrot Juice Recipe

With eight carrots in this recipe, you'll get a large dose of vitamin A and other essential vitamins and minerals your body needs. You get a tangy surprise to this juice by adding the grapefruit. Grapefruits also pack in plenty of great nutrients, such as vitamin C. Some studies even show that grapefruit can even help you boost your weight loss efforts. While the mint is optional in this juice recipe, it really adds to the flavor. Mint also helps to reduce stomach problems and may help prevent cancer as well.

What You'll Need:

2 medium grapefruits
8 unpeeled large carrots
1 mint sprig, fresh (optional)

How to Make It:

Get started by washing the grapefruits, then peeling it and removing any seeds. Break the grapefruits into large sections to make them easily fit into your juicer. Wash the carrots well, but leave the peels on. Take the tops off the carrots as well. Take time to wash the mint before using.

Start by juicing the mint, then run the grapefruit and carrots through the juicer, which should bring out the any mint juice left in the juicer. Serve the juice immediately.

For a nice, refreshing twist, add the juice to a blender, adding in some ice. Blend until you have a slushy mixture. This cold, delicious twist to the juice recipe is wonderful on a very hot day.

Very Veggie Blast Juice Recipe

This juice recipe is packed with many great veggies, including carrots, celery, kale, radishes, tomatoes, bell peppers and more. The apple that is added to the mix adds some sweetness and the fresh ginger root gives the juice a nice kick. You'll get a wide ranges of vitamins and minerals when you whip up this delicious juice recipe.

What You'll Need:

1 red bell pepper
3 celery stalks
1 medium tomato
1 beet
2 inches of turmeric root
½ bunch of kale
2-3 inch chunk of Daikon radish
1 large carrot
3-4 leaves of basil
½ bunch of fresh cilantro
1 green apple
1 inch of fresh ginger root

How to Make It:

Begin by washing the bell pepper, celery stalks, tomato,

beet, kale, radish, carrot, basil leaves, cilantro and apple. Remove seeds and top from the pepper, cutting pepper into large chunks. Chop celery stalks into chunks. Cut the tomato into quarters. Cut the beet into quarters or smaller to make it fit through your juicer. Remove the top of the carrot, but leave peeling on the carrot. Core the green apple and cut into chunks.

Process all the ingredients through a juicer. When juicing is complete, take the leftover pulp and process it in the juicer again. Serve juice right away and avoid saving leftovers.

Bone Building Kale Juice Recipe

Keeping your bones healthy and strong is important, and this juice recipe is packed with great ingredients that include vitamins and minerals that will help keep bones healthy. The kale included in the juice includes vitamin K, vitamin A, vitamin C, iron, calcium and beta carotene. The carrots offer more beta carotene and vitamin A. The apple adds some fiber and sweetness to the juice and even the parsley offers many great health benefits as well.

What You'll Need:

5 large kale leaves
1 medium green apple
5 large carrots
4-6 sprigs of parsley

How to Make It:

Wash the kale leaves and the parsley sprigs and allow them to drain in a colander. Wash the carrots well, removing any dirt. Cut the tops off the carrots but leave the peelings on them. Wash the apple, then core the apple. Leave the apple skin in place, since it includes great nutrients.

Process the kale leaves, green apple, carrots and parsley in the juicer. Cut ingredients into chunks if needed to fit through the juicer. After ingredients are juiced, drink the juice immediately for the best taste and nutritional punch.

*NOTE: a masticating juicer works best for this recipe and others that include leafy greens

Iron Packed Spinach Broccoli Juice Recipe

Getting plenty of iron in your diet is important, since iron helps with the production of red blood cells and the transportation of oxygen throughout your body. If you are not getting enough iron, you could experience symptoms that include headaches, low energy, weak hair and fingernails, shortness of breath and rapid heartbeat. This juice is made with iron packed veggies that help you get a great dose of iron when you drink this juice. Drinking it on a regular basis can help improve your iron levels and the ingredients also provide other important nutrients your body needs as well.

What You'll Need:

2 stalks of broccoli
2 beetroots
8-10 large spinach leaves

How to Make It:

Start by washing the beetroots and the broccoli stalks. Wash the spinach leaves and allow them to drain before juicing. Cut the beetroots and broccoli stalks into large pieces that will go through your juicer.

Juice the ingredients. Enjoy this juice immediately for the best benefits. Makes about 2 servings.

Citrus and Cabbage Juice Recipe

This delicious juice recipe includes a variety of different vegetables and fruits, which means you'll get plenty of nutrients when you drink it. It makes a great juice to start out your day with. The spinach and beetroot offer plenty of iron and the citrus offers a great supply of vitamin C, which helps your body better use the iron. The cabbage included in the juice provides many health benefits as well, including slowing down the aging process and helping to prevent certain types of cancer. All the citrus fruits included in this recipe means you will get a sweet, tangy flavor and you probably will not taste the cabbage and other veggies at all.

What You'll Need:

¼ head of cabbage
5-6 leaves of spinach
1 kiwifruit
½ a large grapefruit
½ of a medium beetroot
1 stalk of broccoli
1 large orange
½ of a large lemon
1 inch piece of fresh ginger

How to Make It:

Wash the cabbage and spinach leaves, allowing them to drain in a colander before juicing. Peel the kiwifruit, grapefruit, orange and lemon. Make sure that you remove any seeds in the grapefruit, orange and lemon. Was the beetroot and broccoli.

Begin by juicing the cabbage, spinach and broccoli. Once they are done juicing, add the ginger and the citrus fruits. When complete, make sure everything is mixed together well. This makes enough juice for at least two servings, so enjoy sharing this juice with a friend or family member instead of saving it.

Cucumber and Tomato Immune Boosting Juice Recipe

Juicing not only provides a great way to lose some weight, but it also can help you boost your immune system as well. This juice in particular is filled with ingredients that will give your immune system a nice boost. The parsley has high iron content and is a great antioxidant that helps to fight off bacteria. The garlic has antibacterial and antiseptic properties, which can boost your immune system as well. Lycopene comes from the tomatoes in the juice, which can help prevent certain types of cancer. While this is not a sweet juice, it has a nice, wholesome, savory taste that you are sure to enjoy.

What You'll Need:

1 large handful of fresh parsley
½ cucumber, unpeeled
2 large tomatoes
1 clove of garlic, peeled
2 stalks of celery
1/8 of a medium sized onion (try a sweet onion like a Vidalia for better flavor)

How to Make It:

Wash the parsley carefully and allow to drain. Wash the cucumber and leave the peeling on, since it includes important nutrients. Wash tomatoes, cutting into large chunks. Peel the garlic clove. Wash celery and onion. Cut celery into chunks.

Add the parsley to the juicer first, since parsley does not provide a whole lot of juice. After juicing the parsley, juice the cucumber, tomatoes, garlic, celery and onion. Pour the mixture into a glass, making sure it is well mixed up. Drink immediate for the best results. Makes a single serving of juice.

Sweet Pineapple Watermelon Juice Recipe

Watermelon is such a sweet, refreshing fruit, especially on a hot day. It is high in vitamin B6, which is known to help reduce tension. If you have a tough day ahead, this juice a great choice. The lemon and pineapple add even more nutrients that are important and plenty of delicious flavor as well. With all the sweetness of this juice, you may want to serve it up over ice for a cool, sweet treat that is actually good for you.

What You'll Need:

¼ of a watermelon
½ of a pineapple
½ of a lemon

How to Make It:

Remove the rind from the watermelon. If the watermelon has seeds, make sure that you remove them before you begin juicing. Remove the rind from the pineapple and peel the lemon. Remove any seeds from the lemon as well. Cut the watermelon and the pineapple into manageable chunks so they are easier for you to juice.

Juice the watermelon, pineapple and lemon. Once you are done juicing, mix the juice well to ensure it is well combined. Drink right away. Serve it over some ice or add it to the blender with a cup or so of ice and blend for a frosty, delicious drink.

Kiwi Strawberry Energy Boosting Juice Recipe

If you need a great boost of energy, try this delicious kiwi strawberry energy boosting juice recipe. It can be a great way to start your day or you can make this juice to drink before you work out. This way you have plenty of energy to help you make the most of your exercise routine. The kiwi, apple, strawberries and lime all give this juice a sweet taste. If you want to make it a little sweeter, you can also mix in just a bit of organic Stevia to the juice before you drink it.

What You'll Need:

½ of a lime
6 large strawberries
4 large kale leaves
2 kiwis, peeled
2 medium green apples
Pinch of organic Stevia (optional)

How to Make It:

Peel the lime and remove and seeds. Wash strawberries, removing the tops. Wash the kale leaves and allow to drain. Wash and peel the kiwis. Wash and then core the apples, leaving on the peels.

Juice the lime, strawberries, kale leaves, kiwis and green apples. Pour into a glass and enjoy this sweet drink right away. Enjoy the natural rush of energy.

Citrus, Apple, Pear Juice Recipe

Pears are a sweet, delicious fruit that happens to be rich in vitamin K, vitamin C and vitamin A. This fruit is also known to help improve digestion, which is important for cleansing out the body. Combined with the tartness of green apples and delicious citrus fruits, this juice will make your taste buds sing. Have fun trying the recipes with several different types of pears, such as red Anjou pears, Bosc pears or the wonderful Asian pears.

What You'll Need:

2 medium pears (choose the pear of your choice)
2 large carrots
1 large orange
1 medium tangerine
1 large granny smith apple

How to Make It:

Wash the pears, removing the core and seeds; however, the peeling can be left on the pears. The carrots should be washed and topped, leaving the peels. Peel the orange and tangerine after washing them, breaking into large sections. Wash and then core the granny smith apple, leaving the peel on the apple as well.

Run the pears, carrots, orange, tangerine and apple through the juicer. Pour the juice over ice and drink it right away. If the juice is too thick or strong, you can always add a bit of water to get the juice to your desired consistency and taste.

Beta Carotene Deluxe Juice Recipe

You are guaranteed to get a huge dose of beta carotene when you drink this delicious juice. It includes delicious cantaloupe, which is known to include many different vitamins and minerals essential to your body. Vitamin C and vitamin A are just a few of the important vitamins included in cantaloupe. You will also find that it includes a high concentration of potassium as well.

What You'll Need:

1 medium cantaloupe
4 medium sized carrots
1 large sweet potato

How to Make It:

Wash the cantaloupe and then remove the rind. However, you should try to leave a bit of the greenish rind behind to juice, since it offers many great nutrients. Wash the carrots and top them, leaving the peelings. Wash the sweet potato thoroughly, leaving the peel on the sweet potato as well.

Juice the cantaloupe, carrots and sweet potato. Make sure the juice is well mixed to combine the flavors. Drink immediate for a large amount of beta carotene.

Antioxidant Mixed Berry Juice Recipe

When it comes to getting antioxidants, berries happen to have more antioxidants than most other fruits. Antioxidants found in the berries help to protect the body against damage from free radicals. Many berries can also aid in weight loss, since raspberries are known to include ketones that help burn off fat and strawberries can help keep blood sugar levels stable. Strawberries include more than 100% of the daily value of vitamin C and other berries like blackberries and blueberries include a high amount of vitamin C as well. The addition of mango to this juice recipe adds even more vitamin C and a nice dose of vitamin A as well. The apples add some great fiber, which will fill you up and help keep your digestive system working the way it should. This juice will taste wonderful when blended with some ice or simply served over ice, offering a chilly, refreshing, healthy drink that will taste great at any time of day.

What You'll Need:

1 cup of blueberries
1 cup of strawberries
½ cup of raspberries
½ cup of blackberries

½ cup of cubed mango

1 green apple

How to Make It:

Wash the blueberries, strawberries, raspberries and blackberries. Remove the stems from the strawberries. Wash a mango and peel it, cubing up a ½ cup of the mango. Save the rest of the mango for another juicing recipe. Wash the apple and then core it and remove its seeds. Leave the apple peeling in place.

Pass the blueberries, strawberries, raspberries, blackberries, mango and apple through a juicer. Juice the apple last, since it will help clean out some of the berry juices left behind. Pour over ice or mix in a blender with a cup of ice. Drink immediately for a nice dose of antioxidants.

Coconut Mango Tropical Delight Juice Recipe

Mangos have a delicious, sweet flavor. Not only do they taste great, but they include high amounts of vitamin C and pectin as well, which can help lower blood pressure and cholesterol. The vitamin A included in mangos can help keep eyes healthy as well. The one problem people often have with mangos is figuring out if they are ripe or not. A ripe mango should have a bit of give to the outside skin and should have a nice, sweet scent as well. The addition of coconut water and several tropical fruits makes this juice recipe a delight for your taste buds.

What You'll Need:

1 large mango, prepared
2 medium oranges
2 cups of pineapple, cubed
1 lime
½ inch piece of fresh ginger
Coconut water, to your own taste

How to Make It:

To prepare the mango for juicing, start by washing the skin carefully to ensure the flesh is not contaminated. The pit must be removed from the mango, which can be done by slicing around the pit and pulling sections apart to pop out the pit. Use a sharp knife to score the mango flesh, then scooping out the flesh with a spoon, ensuring the rind is left behind.

Wash and peel the oranges and ensure pineapple is cubed small enough to easily go through the juicer. Peel the lime and remove any seeds. Wash ginger before juicing as well.

Run the mango flesh, oranges, pineapple, lime and ginger through the juicer. Mix the finished juice with some coconut water until you have the flavor you prefer. Drink at room temperature or pour over ice for a refreshing tropical treat.

Pear, Apple, Blueberry Juice Recipe

Blueberries are not just wonderfully juicy and sweet, but these small berries include a high amount of antioxidants as well. This fruit is known to help reduce the risk of inflammation and may help protect against certain types of cancer as well. Since these berries have such thin skin, it is a good idea to use organic berries whenever possible. This juice recipe adds the delicate flavor of pears and the sweet, tartness of granny smith apples as well, making a juice that is packed with flavor and great nutrients for the body. Enjoy changing up the flavor a bit by using different kinds of pears in the juice.

What You'll Need:

1 cup of blueberries
½ cup of strawberries
½ cup of blackberries
1 pear, any kind
2 granny smith apples

How to Make It:

Wash the blueberries, strawberries and blackberries. Remove the tops from the strawberries. Wash the pear and the apple. Remove the core and stem from the pear, cutting the pear into large chunks. Core the apple, leave the skin on and then cut the apple into large pieces.

Run the blueberries, strawberries and blackberries through the juicer first. Then, run the pear and apples through the juicer, cleaning out the berry juices when they go through the juicer. Fill a glass with ice cubes and pour juice over the ice. Drink the juice right away to get the most nutrients from the ingredients.

Carrot and Cucumber Broccoli Juice Recipe

The broccoli included in this juice is high in both vitamin C and vitamin E, which are known to help support the immune system. This vegetable also has anti-carcinogenic properties and some evidence shows that broccoli may help prevent cancer. Although broccoli offers great nutrition, it is low in calories, which means it is a great addition to your juices if you are trying to lose weight. When juicing the broccoli, make sure you juice the head and the stalks for the nutrition. The carrots and cucumbers add more flavor and nutrition to this juice.

What You'll Need:

1 large cucumber
3 stalks of celery, including the leaves
1 stalk of broccoli, including the head and the stalk
3 large carrots

How to Make It:

Begin by washing the cucumber, celery and carrots. Clean the broccoli very well, since the head often traps bacteria and dirt. Leave the peeling on the cucumber and cut into large chunks. Cut the celery into chunks as well. Do not peel the carrots, but make sure you remove the tops, then cutting the carrots into large pieces. Cut the broccoli into small enough pieces to easily fit into your juicer.

Run the cucumber, celery, broccoli and carrots through your juicer. When done juicing, serve up the juice right away. This juice is usually best at room temperature.

Delicious Tropical Papaya and Pineapple Juice Recipe

Since pineapple has such a high water content, it is a great fruit to use when juicing, providing plenty of juice. Pineapple is high in minerals like manganese and vitamins, such as vitamin C. The sweetness of the pineapple is delicious with other fruits that are more tart. To get the most out of your pineapple when juicing, add the core of the pineapple to the juicer as well, since it offers a lot of bromelain. The other tropical fruits in this juice, such as the papaya, guava and mango, really add a complexity of flavors to this juice.

What You'll Need:

1 large orange, peeled
1 cup of papaya, cubed
1 cup of pineapple, cubed
1 guava
½ of a large mango

How to Make It:

Rinse off the orange and then peel it, removing any seeds. Break the orange up into large sections. Prepare a papaya and cube up a cup of it for the juice. Cube up a cup of pineapple, including some of the core. Prepare the guava for juicing. Wash the mango, removing the pit and using half of the mango flesh for this recipe. Save the rest of the mango for another juice recipe.

Run the orange, papaya, pineapple, guava and mango through the juicer. Fill a large glass with crushed ice, pouring the juice over the ice. Serve the juice immediately for the best flavor and nutrition. This juice is so delicious that you may want to double the recipe and share some with a friend.

Pineapple and Kale Detoxifying Juice Recipe

This recipe includes all the benefits of pineapple, including bromelain, vitamin C and manganese. It also includes great nutrition from the kale included, as well as wonderful nutrients from the cucumber, lemon and mint. This juice is a great detoxifying recipe. For the best results, make this recipe and drink the juice throughout an entire day. Refrigerate the juice until needed but make sure all the juice is consumed within 24 hours or less.

What You'll Need:

2 large cucumbers, unpeeled
½ of a lemon, peeled and seeded
½ cup of pineapple, including the core
1 large bunch of mint
1 large bunch of kale, stems removed
¼ inch of fresh ginger

How to Make It:

Rinse the cucumber thoroughly, leaving the peelings in place. Chunk the cucumbers into large pieces. Wash the lemon, peel it and then remove any seeds. Prepare the pineapple, ensuring it is cubed and include a bit of the core with the pineapple chunks. Wash the mint leaves and kale in a colander, allowing to drain thoroughly before juicing. Wash the ginger as well.

Process the cucumbers, lemon, pineapple, mint, kale and ginger in the juicer. Place the juice in a pitcher. Drink one cup of the juice right away. Store leftovers in the refrigerator and consume throughout the day. Ensure all the juice is consumed within one day for the best results.

Fruity Cleansing Juice Recipe

Many people choose to go on the juicing diet to cleanse their body and lose weight. While there are many delicious juicing recipes that can be used to accomplish these goals, this fruity cleansing recipe is a delicious, nutritious way to begin cleansing the body. All the fruits included provide plenty of vitamins and minerals, not to mention you are sure to appreciate the delicious, fruity flavor as well.

What You'll Need:

1 granny smith apple
½ cup of blueberries
½ cup of raspberries
2 large peaches
2 large oranges, peeled

How to Make It:

To begin making the fruity cleansing juice recipe, start by washing the granny smith apple, the blueberries, raspberries, peaches and oranges. After all the fruits have been washed, remove the core and seeds from the apple, leaving the peeling intact. Remove the seeds from the peaches, but leave the peach skins intact. Peel the oranges, removing any seeds. Cut the apple and peaches into large pieces and break the oranges into large sections.

Process the blueberries, raspberries, peaches and oranges in a juicer. Run the apple pieces through the juicer last. Drink the juice right away. For the best cleansing results, drink the juice while it is at room temperature.

Go Green Spinach and Cucumber Juice Recipe

This delicious juice recipe is all about the greens. It has cucumbers, parsley, spinach, celery and even a granny smith apple in it. All the spinach offers a great dose of potassium and iron. Not only does this juice provide many essential vitamins and minerals that your body needs, but also the juice is also great for detoxifying your body. If you do not like the flavor, you can always add a second apple to the recipe to add some extra sweetness.

What You'll Need:

2 large handfuls of baby spinach
1 stalk of celery, with the leaves
1 large cucumber
1 large handful of fresh parsley
1 large granny smith apple

How to Make It:

Use a colander and rinse the baby spinach and parsley, allowing the leaves to drain in the colander until they are well drained. Wash the celery, cucumber and the apple. Chop the celery into large pieces. Leave the peeling on the cucumber and chop it into large chunks.

Core the apple, making sure all seeds are removed. Do not remove the peel. Cut the apple into pieces.

Run the spinach and parsley through the juicer first, since they do not provide as much juice. Then, run the celery, cucumber and apple through the juicer last. Blend together all the juices. Serve this juice over some ice in a tall glass. Enjoy immediately.

Spinach and Cinnamon Metabolism Booster Juice Recipe

If you are juicing for weight loss, you want to consume juices that will give your metabolism a nice boost. After all, if you have been eating processed foods for many years, your metabolism may have slowed down, which can make it more difficult for you to lose weight. This recipe will help give your metabolism a nice boost and it is packed with ingredients that help to blast away fat as well. The cinnamon adds a nice touch to the juice and is known to help stabilize blood sugar levels.

What You'll Need:

1 cup of spinach leaves
4 large carrots, unpeeled
1 lemon
1 stalk of celery with the leaves
¼ teaspoon of cinnamon
1 granny smith green apple

How to Make It:

Start out by placing the spinach leaves in a colander, rinsing them very well before using. Allow to drain a bit before juicing them. Wash the carrots, topping them but leaving the peelings on them. The lemon should be peeled and the seeds removed after washing it. Wash the celery and apple as well. Cut the celery into big pieces. Core the apple and then cut into pieces too.

Run the spinach leaves from the juicer first. Then run the carrots, celery, lemon and apple through your juicer. After juicing, mix the cinnamon into the juice, stirring well to combine. If the lemon makes the juice a bit tart, use a bit of purified water to dilute it a bit before drinking. Drink right away and enjoy the boost to your metabolism.

Green Juice with a Hint of Sweetness Recipe

This is a green juice recipe that includes all green ingredients. While it includes greens like kale, romaine and parsley, the apple adds a touch of sweetness to the juice. With all the greens in the juice, this is a drink that is packed with vitamins and minerals that will fuel your body and offer plenty of energy for your day. Try drinking this juice if you are feeling a bit tired or you feel like your immune system needs a boost.

What You'll Need:

3 stalks of celery
2 cups of fresh parsley
1 granny smith apple
2 cups of kale leaves
1 large cucumber
3 cups of romaine lettuce

How to Make It:

The celery, cucumber and apple should all be washed. The parsley, kale and romaine leaves can be washed in a colander and allowed to drain and dry a bit before you place them in a juicer.

Cut the celery and cucumber into chunks, leaving the peeling on the cucumber. Do not peel the apple, but core it and then cut into large apple chunks.

Process the parsley, kale leaves and romaine lettuce in the juicer first. Then run the celery, apple and cucumber through the juicer. Make sure you mix up the juicer very well to ensure you get the hint of sweetness throughout the entire batch of juice. Serve the juice immediately.

Potassium Delight Spinach Juice Recipe

Potassium is an important nutrient that your body needs. If you do not get enough potassium, you may suffer from muscle cramps and other symptoms. This juice can help you ensure that you are getting enough potassium in your diet, since the spinach is extremely high in potassium. The lemon juice adds some great flavor to the juice.

What You'll Need:

1 granny smith or other green apple
1 stalk of celery
1 handful of fresh baby spinach leaves
4 medium carrots, tops and greens removed
½ lemon
1 handful of fresh parsley

How to Make It:

Thoroughly rinse off the apple, celery, carrots and lemon. Use a colander to rinse the baby spinach leaves and parsley, letting the leaves dry some before using them in the juice. Without removing the peeling, core the apple and cut into quarters. Cut the celery into large pieces. Remove the carrot tops and chop carrots into big chunks. Peel the lemon and ensure any seeds have been removed before juicing.

Juice the parsley and the spinach leaves first. Place the apple, celery, lemon and carrots in the juicer. Juice. Ensure the juice is well mixed together for the best flavor. Serve the juice right away.

V-8 Flavored Juice Recipe

If you like the flavor of V-8 juice, this juice recipe is a great choice for you to try. You get the great flavor of the juice with even more vegetables and you can be sure of the ingredients going into the juice. With all the great vegetables in this juice, it has plenty of great flavor. The hot sauce really adds a nice pop to the juice, although it is optional and you do not have to add it if you do not like hot sauce. Whip this juice up on a hot day and enjoy the taste of vegetable goodness while getting all those important vitamins and other needed nutrients.

What You'll Need:

2 large tomatoes
2 medium carrots
2 teaspoons of lemon juice
¼ cup of water
1 large handful of spinach leaves
2 stalks of celery
2 cloves of garlic
¼ of a sweet Vidalia onion or other sweet onion
Hot sauce to taste (optional)

How to Make It:

Thoroughly wash the tomatoes, carrots, celery and onion. Rinse leaves well within a colander and let them drain. Peel the garlic cloves. Chop tomatoes into quarters or eights, making sure they will fit in the juicers. Chop the carrots, celery and onion into large chunks.

Place the spinach in the juicer and process. Add the tomatoes, carrots, celery, garlic and onion in the juicer and juice. Once the juice is complete, add the lemon juice and water. Mix together until well combined. Add the hot sauce to the juice to your own taste. Serve the juice right away and enjoy the nice combination of vegetable flavors.

Blueberry and Pomegranate Fruit Juice Recipe

Pomegranates are very high in antioxidants and vitamins, such as vitamin C. This fruit is known to help lower cholesterol and reduce the risk of heart disease. While pomegranates are delicious, preparing them for juicing can be a bit perplexing. Instead of eating the flesh of the pomegranate, the seeds of the fruit are actually eaten instead. This juice recipe not only includes pomegranates, but it includes blueberries and grapes as well, which add even more vitamins and antioxidants to this incredibly healthy and delicious juice. The wonderful sweetness makes it a great juice to enjoy when you want something sweet and refreshing.

What You'll Need:

1 cup of fresh organic blueberries
2 cups of red grapes
1 pomegranate, only the seeds

How to Make It:

To prepare the pomegranate, start by cutting the knob off the top of the fruit. Then use a very sharp knife to score the fruit, scoring in quarters. Pull away the sections of the rind. Hold the rind over cold water, popping the seeds off the rind. In the cold water, use your fingers to get the membranes off the seeds. Do this gently to avoid damaging the seeds. Simply allow the pith to go to the top of the water and remove it. Drain the seeds.

Wash the blueberries and the grapes thoroughly in a colander before you juice them, even if they are organic.

Place the pomegranate seeds in the juicer first, juicing them. Then process the blueberries and the red grapes, juicing them. Mix the juices together when complete. Pour the juice over some ice and enjoy right away.

Pumpkin Pineapple Juice Recipe

If you are making juices during the fall, you will definitely want to give this recipe a try, since pumpkins are more readily available during the fall months. Pumpkins offer excellent nutrition and they are very rich in vitamins like vitamin C and vitamin A. These vitamins can help to keep skin healthy, prevent aging and keep your immune system strong. The addition of pineapple and apples to this juice gives it a tropical flavor and the spices really give the juice a great taste.

What You'll Need:

½ cup of pineapple chunks
1 small pumpkin
2 green apples, such as granny smith
¼ teaspoon of allspice
¼ teaspoon of ginger
Purified water to taste

How to Make It:

Make sure the pumpkin is washed before you begin working with it. Then you will want cut the top off the pumpkin, scooping out the pumpkin flesh. Make sure you remove the seeds from the pumpkin flesh and do not put the pumpkin rind in the juicer.

Wash the apples and then core them to ensure all the seeds are removed. Leave the peelings on the apples.

Run the pumpkin flesh through the juicer. If you have a lot of pulp left, you can run it through the juicer again to extract more juice. Then, juice the pineapple and the apples. Mix the juices all together. Add the allspice and the ginger to the juice, mixing to combine. Add purified water to the juice until you have a flavor you enjoy. Drink the juice right away.

Body Cleansing Celery Juice Recipe

Celery is a great ingredient for cleaning out your body. It has a lot of water in it, which helps cleanse out the body. While this juice will help cleanse your body, it also contains some great nutrients from the spinach included. The beet included is a great cleansing ingredient as well. Drink this juice and enjoy getting a nice cleanse, which will help you lose weight and feel healthier. While the juice does have a very strong green taste to it, it really works so give it a try.

What You'll Need:

1 bunch of fresh cilantro
4 stalks of celery with the leaves
1 large handful of spinach
½ a beet

How to Make It:

Wash the beet and the celery stalks carefully. Cut the celery and the ½ a beet into pieces so they can be easily juiced. Place the cilantro and the spinach in a large colander, running water over them to rinse the leaves well. Allow to drain for a few minutes before you begin juicing.

Process the cilantro and the spinach through the juicer first. Last, add the celery and beet to the juicer, juicing until complete. Make sure that you mix the juices together very well to combined the flavors. Place in a glass and drink right away. If you are not fond of the flavor, try drinking it quickly while it is lukewarm to quickly get it down.

Chapter 5: Your 7 Day Juicing Diet Meal Plan

As you go on your juicing diet, you may be a bit unfamiliar with how to get started. To help you more easily begin the juicing diet, we've developed a helpful 7-day juicing diet meal plan to help you through those first days. Keep in mind, after a few days of juicing, you should go back to a regular diet. Juicing long term is usually unhealthy. However, even after you spend some time on the juicing diet, you can continue to use these recipes to replace a meal during your day as you continue to lead a healthy lifestyle. These juices are also great if your body is feeling a bit down and you want to get a large dose of great nutrients that your body needs. Begin your diet using this meal plan for great results. Feel free to mix and match days up if you want to keep things interesting and to your own unique taste.

Day 1:

Breakfast: Pineapple and Kale Detoxifying Juice Recipe

Lunch: Carrot and Cucumber Broccoli Juice Recipe

Dinner: Go Green Spinach and Cucumber Juice Recipe

Day 2:

Breakfast: Fruity Cleansing Juice Recipe

Lunch: Potassium Delight Spinach Juice Recipe

Dinner: Citrus and Cabbage Juice Recipe

Day 3:

Breakfast: Delicious Tropical Papaya and Pineapple Juice Recipe

Lunch: Iron Packed Spinach Broccoli Juice Recipe

Dinner: Green Juice with a Hint of Sweetness Recipe

Day 4:

Breakfast: Pear, Apple, Blueberry Juice Recipe

Lunch: Sweet Pineapple Watermelon Juice Recipe

Dinner: V-8 Flavored Juice Recipe

Day 5:

Breakfast: Coconut Mango Tropical Delight Juice Recipe

Lunch: Spinach and Cinnamon Metabolism Booster Juice Recipe

Dinner: Pumpkin Pineapple Juice Recipe

Day 6:

Breakfast: Blueberry and Pomegranate Fruit Juice Recipe

Lunch: Beta Carotene Deluxe Juice Recipe

Dinner: Cucumber and Tomato Immune Boosting Juice Recipe

Day 7:

Breakfast: Body Cleansing Celery Juice Recipe

Lunch: Antioxidant Mixed Berry Juice Recipe

Dinner: Citrus, Apple, Pear Juice Recipe

Printed in Great Britain
by Amazon.co.uk, Ltd.,
Marston Gate.